Kitchen Design

teNeues

Imprint

Produced by fusion publishing GmbH, Berlin   www.fusion-publishing.com

Bettina Schlösser (Editorial Coordination teNeues)
Lea Bauer (Editorial Coordination)
Nicolas Uphaus (Text); Sabine Scholz (Text Coordination)
Wohanka & Kollegen GmbH (Translations)
Janine Minkner, Manuela Roth (Layout); Jan Hausberg (Imaging & Pre-press)

Photos (page): courtesy AEG – Electrolux (AEG – Electrolux, pages 174, 192, 194), courtesy Alno AG (Alno, pages 18-25, 72-81, 206, 212-214, 217), courtesy Ballerina-Küchen (Ballerina-Küchen, pages 26-31, 82-91, 186, 216), courtesy Bulthaup GmbH & Co. KG (Bulthaup, pages 9, 10, 12, 15, 92-107, 164, 180, 182-185, 187, 200-202, 207, 215), courtesy cucina GmbH (cucina, pages 108-117), courtesy Gaggenau Hausgeräte GmbH (Gaggenau, pages 11, 166-171, 195), courtesy IKEA Deutschland GmbH & Co. KG (IKEA, pages 32-37, 118-125, 199), courtesy Kornmüller GesmbH & CoKG (Kornmüller, pages 7, 56-61, 64-71), courtesy Miele & Cie. KG (Miele, pages 172, 175-179, 181, 188, 193, 196), courtesy Poggenpohl Möbelwerke GmbH (Poggenpohl, pages 62, 126-135, 218-221), courtesy rational einbauküchen GmbH (rational, pages 4, 13, 38-49, 136-147, 190), courtesy SieMatic Deutschland (SieMatic, pages 3, 6, 8, 14, 16, 50-55, 148-157, 198, 203-205, 208-211), courtesy TEAM 7 Natürlich Wohnen GmbH (TEAM 7, pages 5, 158-163)

Cover photo: courtesy Poggenpohl Möbelwerke GmbH (Poggenpohl)
Back cover photos from top to bottom: courtesy Bulthaup GmbH & Co. KG (Bulthaup); courtesy Ballerina-Küchen (Ballerina-Küchen); courtesy IKEA Deutschland GmbH & Co. KG (IKEA); courtesy Bulthaup GmbH & Co. KG (Bulthaup); courtesy SieMatic Deutschland (SieMatic)

Published by teNeues Publishing Group

teNeues Verlag GmbH + Co. KG
Am Selder 37
47906 Kempen, Germany
Tel.: 0049-(0)2152-916-0
Fax: 0049-(0)2152-916-111
E-mail: books@teneues.de

teNeues Publishing Company
16 West 22nd Street
New York, NY 10010, USA
Tel.: 001-212-627-9090
Fax: 001-212-627-9511

teNeues Publishing UK Ltd.
York Villa, York Road
Byfleet
KT14 7HX, Great Britain
Tel.: 0044-1932-403509
Fax: 0044-1932-403514

teNeues France S.A.R.L.
93, rue Bannier
45000 Orléans, France
Tel.: 0033-2-38541071
Fax: 0033-2-38625340

Press department: arehn@teneues.de
Tel.: 0049-2152-916-202

www.teneues.com

ISBN: 978-3-8327-9338-8

Bibliographic information published by the Deutsche Nationalbibliothek.
The Deutsche Nationalbibliothek lists this publication in the Deutsche Nationalbibliografie; detailed bibliographic data are available in the Internet at http://dnb.d-nb.de.

CLASSIC KITCHENS

MODERN KITCHENS

ELEMENTS

Introduction

The kitchen is the heart of every home. It is the cozy room where you cook, bake and eat together. In the past, kitchens tended to be small rooms with the emphasis on function, solely there for the preparation of food. Today, kitchen requirements have changed significantly: generously-sized rooms are in demand that fuse together the kitchen and living area, creating comfortable and inviting spaces that can be enjoyed by family and friends.

Kitchen manufacturers now offer the right solution for every requirement, from generously-sized and luxurious to compact and sophisticated, allowing the customer to individually design their personal dream kitchen. Precious materials with easy-to-clean surfaces support the clear, geometrical layouts and well thought-out details create storage space allowing for more accessibility.

Sophisticated electric equipment for cooling, cooking and baking perform their jobs increasingly more efficiently. And multimedia found its way into the modern kitchen with music, TV and Internet seamlessly integrated into components that help to support one's lifestyle.

Nicolas Uphaus

Einleitung

Die Küche ist das Herz eines jeden Hauses. Hier wird gekocht, gebacken, gespeist und gemütlich zusammengesessen. Waren Küchen vor einigen Jahren eher kleine, möglichst funktionale Räume, die allein der Essenszubereitung dienten, so haben sich die Ansprüche inzwischen deutlich gewandelt: Großzügigkeit ist gefragt und der Zusammenschluss von Küche und Wohnbereich ergibt eine behagliche und kommunikative Einheit, die mit Familie und Freunden genossen wird.

Die Küchenhersteller bieten für jeden Anspruch die richtige Lösung. Ob großzügig und luxuriös oder kompakt und raffiniert – der Kunde kann seine persönliche Traumküche ganz individuell gestalten. Edle und zugleich pflegeleichte Oberflächen unterstützen das klare, geometrische Layout und durchdachte Details schaffen Stauraum und erhöhen die Funktionalität.

Elektrogeräte zum Kühlen, Kochen und Backen verrichten ihren Dienst immer effizienter und raffinierter. Längst hat auch das Thema Multimedia Einzug in die moderne Küche gehalten: Musik, TV und Internet sind nahtlos in die Komponenten integriert und erweitern Funktionalität und Unterhaltungswert.

Nicolas Uphaus

Introduction

La cuisine est le cœur de chaque maison. On cuisine, on cuit, on mange et on s'installe confortablement tous ensembles pour un repas dans cette pièce. Si les cuisines d'il y a quelques années étaient des pièces assez petites et les plus fonctionnelles possibles, ne servant qu'à la préparation des repas, les exigences ont bien changées entre temps pour en arriver à celles-ci : elles doivent être généreuses, et la fusion de la cuisine avec l'espace de vie produit une unité confortable et communicative appréciée par la famille comme par les amis.

Les fabricants de cuisine offre une solution à chaque exigence. Généreuse et luxueuse ou compacte et raffinée, le client peut aménager la cuisine de ses rêves. Des surfaces superbes mais néanmoins faciles d'entretien renforcent l'aspect net et géométrique, et des détails bien pensés offrent des espaces de rangement et une fonctionnalité accrue.

Les appareils électroménagers pour réfrigérer, cuire et cuisiner effectuent leur tâche avec toujours plus d'efficacité et de façon toujours plus raffinée. Depuis un certain temps, le thème multimédia a également fait son apparition dans la cuisine moderne : la musique, la télévision et l'internet sont aisément intégrés dans les composants et élargissent la fonctionnalité et la capacité de distraction.

Nicolas Uphaus

Introducción

La cocina es el centro en cada casa. Allí se cocina, se hornea, se degusta y se come en familia. Si hace algunos años las cocinas fueron más bien un cuarto pequeño y lo más funcional posible, que solamente servía para preparar la comida, entretanto han cambiado considerablemente las exigencias: está en boga la generosidad y la unión de la cocina y la sala de estar da como resultado una unidad agradable y comunicativa que se disfruta con la familia y los amigos.

Los fabricantes de cocinas ofrecen la solución correcta para cada exigencia. Ya sea amplia y lujosa o compacta y sofisticada —el cliente puede diseñar su cocina de ensueño de manera muy individual. Las superficies nobles y fáciles de cuidar a la vez, apoyan a la distribución geométrica clara, y los detalles bien concebidos logran capacidad para guardar cosas y aumentan la funcionalidad.

Los electrodomésticos para enfriar, cocinar y hornear funcionan cada vez más eficiente y sofisticadamente. Hace tiempo que el tema multimedia ya entró a la cocina moderna: la música, la televisión e internet están integrados perfectamente en los componentes y amplían la funcionalidad y el entretenimiento.

Nicolas Uphaus

Introduzione

La cucina rappresenta il cuore di ogni casa. Qui si cucina, si inforna, si degustano le pietanze e ci si intrattiene a tavola insieme. Mentre nel passato le cucine erano per lo più ambienti piccoli, possibilmente funzionali, adatti solo alla mera preparazione di pietanze, le esigenze sono cambiate notevolmente nel frattempo: è richiesto molto più spazio, ed il collegamento tra la cucina e la zona giorno costituisce un'unità confortevole e comunicativa, da vivere appieno con la famiglia e con gli amici.

I costruttori di cucine propongono la soluzione perfetta per ogni esigenza. Una versione ampia e preziosa, oppure compatta e raffinata – il Cliente può realizzare in un modo molto personalizzato il suo sogno personale di cucina. Le superfici preziose, ma perfettamente robuste e resistenti, sottolineano il chiaro design delle geometrie e dei dettagli raffinati, danno vita allo spazio per riporre alimenti ed utensili ed elevano la funzionalità dell'intero complesso.

Gli elettrodomestici per refrigerare, cucinare ed infornare svolgono la loro funzione in modo sempre più efficiente e raffinato. Già da molto tempo, la cucina è arricchita anche con le moderne tecnologie multimediali: impianti audio, televisori e internet sono stati integrati ai suoi componenti, donando maggiore funzionalità e potenziale di intrattenimento.

Nicolas Uphaus

CLASSIC KITCHENS

In these models, modern comfort is achieved by the large-scale use of wood and wood impressions for cabinets and countertops. Combined with friendly colors and clear lines these are the ideal conditions for creating an open-plan kitchen linked to the living area.

Moderne Wohnlichkeit wird hier durch den großflächigen Einsatz von Holz und Holzanmutungen für Fronten und auch bei Arbeitsflächen erreicht. In Verbindung mit freundlichen Farben und klaren Linien ist dies die beste Voraussetzung, um durch einen offenen Übergang die Küche mit dem Wohnbereich zu verbinden.

Un confort moderne est atteint grâce aux grandes surfaces en bois et à l'imitation de l'aspect du bois sur les façades, ainsi que sue le plan de travail. En relation avec des couleurs chaleureuses et des lignes nettes, c'est là la meilleure façon de réunir la cuisine et l'espace de vie.

El confort moderno se logra gracias al uso de grandes superficies de madera y aspectos de madera para frentes y también en superficies de trabajo. En combinación con colores agradables y líneas claras, este es el mejor requisito para unir la cocina con la sala de estar con un paso abierto.

Il concetto di accoglienza, inteso in chiave moderna, è dato qui dal generoso impiego del legno e dell'effetto legno per le ante ed i piani di lavoro. Grazie all'associazione di tinte cromatiche gradevoli e linee definite, si ottiene la premessa migliore per annettere la cucina alla zona giorno, attraverso un passaggio senza barriere oggettive.

Alno

Muted warm colors combined with a clean layout of different elements provide a cozy, while at the same time structured, environment. The kitchen's functional and sturdy working environment can thus be directly integrated into the living area, turning the kitchen into the centre of the living space.

Gedeckte, warme Farben in Verbindung mit einer klaren Anordnung der verschiedenen Elemente sorgen für eine gemütliche und zugleich strukturierte Umgebung. Die funktionale und strapazierfähige Arbeitsumgebung der Küche kann so direkt in den Wohnbereich eingebunden werden und die Küche zum Zentrum des Lebensraums machen.

Des couleurs chaudes et discrètes, ainsi qu'un aménagement clair des divers éléments assurent un environnement à la fois confortable et structuré. Le cadre de travail fonctionnel et résistant peut ainsi être intégré directement dans le salon, de sorte que la cuisine devienne le centre de l'espace de vie.

Los colores apagados y cálidos junto a una disposición clara de los diferentes elementos proporcionan un ambiente agradable y estructurado a la vez. Así se puede incluir el ambiente de trabajo funcional y resistente de la cocina directamente en la sala de estar y convertir la cocina en el centro del espacio vital.

I colori caldi ed accoglienti, collegati ad una chiara successione dei diversi elementi, generano un ambiente gradevole, ma allo stesso tempo perfettamente strutturato. Lo spazio di lavoro della cucina, funzionale e resistente, può così essere direttamente integrato alla zona giorno, rendendo la cucina il centro effettivo della propria casa.

Ballerina-Küchen

These classic kitchen ranges are clean and yet comfortable—whether in subtle country house style or rather stark with a strong color accent. Something special about the "Bravad" model (pp. 40–41) is that the individual modules can be flexibly positioned in the room and combined with each other.

Klar und trotzdem wohnlich kommen diese klassischen Küchenmodelle daher – ob im dezenten Landhausstil oder eher sachlich, mit kräftigem Farbakzent. Eine Besonderheit des Modells „Bravad" (S. 40–41) ist, dass die einzelnen Module sich flexibel im Raum positionieren und miteinander kombinieren lassen.

Ces modèles de cuisine classiques sont clairs, mais néanmoins agréables, qu'ils soient dans un style discret de maison de campagne ou avec de puissants accents colorés. Une particularité du modèle « Bravad » (p. 40–41) est que les modules peuvent se positionner dans la pièce de façon flexible, ou être combinés.

Claros y de todas maneras acogedores, ya sea en estilo campestre o más bien sobrio con acento intenso de color, estos modelos clásicos de cocina están disponibles. Una particularidad del modelo "Bravad" (p. 40–41) es que cada uno de los modelos se pueden colocar y combinar flexiblemente en el ambiente.

Questi modelli classici di cucina sono chiari, ma allo stesso tempo accoglienti – sia nel delicato stile rustico, sia nel design molto più eccentrico, caratterizzato da note cromatiche intense. Una delle particolarità del modello "Bravad" (p. 40–41) è data dai singoli moduli, in grado di combinarsi nello spazio l'uno con l'altro con la massima flessibilità.

IKEA

These kitchen models, as different as they all are, are based on country house style inspired by different regions. Classic elements like paneled doors and subtle decorations are combined with precious woods and friendly colors.

Diese Küchenmodelle setzen alle, so verschieden sie sind, auf einen von unterschiedlichen Regionen inspirierten Landhausstil. Klassische Elemente wie Kassettentüren und dezente Verzierungen werden kombiniert mit edlen Hölzern und freundlichen Farben.

Tous ces modèles de cuisine, bien que très différents, sont inspirés de styles de maison de campagne de diverses régions. Des éléments classiques tels que des portes cassettes et des ornementations discrètes sont combinés à des bois précieux et des couleurs chaleureuses.

A pesar de ser tan diferentes, todos los modelos de cocinas apuestan por un estilo campestre inspirado en varias regiones. Los elementos clásicos, tales como puertas artesonadas y ornamentos decentes, se combinan con maderas nobles y colores agradables.

Questi modelli di cucine sono tutti, sebbene così diversi tra di loro, il risultato di uno stile rustico ispirato da diverse regioni. Gli elementi classici, quali le ante con telaio in rilievo e le delicate decorazioni, sono qui associati a legni preziosi e colori armoniosi.

rational

This range focuses on the combination of different classic styles with professional elements from which the customer can put together their own very personal kitchen. Developed in collaboration with the American designer Mick De Giulio, it goes beyond nostalgica.

In dieser Serie wird auf die Verbindung von verschiedenen klassischen Stilen mit professionellen Elementen gesetzt, aus denen der Kunde seine ganz persönliche Küche zusammenstellen kann. In Zusammenarbeit mit dem amerikanischen Designer Mick De Giulio entwickelt, bedient sie jedoch nicht nur die Vorstellungen von Nostalgikern.

Cette série mise sur la réunion de divers styles classiques avec des éléments professionnels que le client peut choisir pour confectionner sa cuisine personnelle. Développée en collaboration avec le designer américain Mick De Giulio, elle ne satisfera cependant pas que les idées des nostalgiques.

En esta serie se apuesta por la combinación de los diferentes estilos clásicos con elementos profesionales, de los cuales el cliente puede crear su cocina muy personal. Desarrollada en cooperación con el diseñador americano Mick De Giulio, no solamente satisface las ideas de nostálgicos.

In questa serie, è posto un particolare accento sull'unione di stili classici diversi con degli elementi professionali, attraverso i quali il Cliente può elaborare la sua cucina molto personalizzata. La serie, realizzata in collaborazione con il designer americano Mick De Giulio, non è però solo per i nostalgici dello stile classico.

SieMatic

Surfaces in warm brown and earth tones characterize these kitchens and create a cozy but jet functional atmosphere. With the "Pisa" model (pp. 68–69) characteristic round windows allow a glance into the cupboards and provide a distinctive impression.

Oberflächen in warmen Braun- und Erdtönen prägen diese Küchen und schaffen so eine behagliche Atmosphäre bei gleichzeitiger Funktionalität. Beim Modell „Pisa" (S. 68–69) erlauben charakteristische runde Fenster einen Blick in die Schränke und sorgen für eine unverwechselbare Anmutung.

De nombreuses surfaces dans les tons bruns et terre confèrent à cette cuisine une atmosphère confortable tout en étant fonctionnelle. Dans le modèle « Pisa » (p. 68–69), des fenêtres rondes caractéristiques offrent un aperçu du contenu des placards et assurent un aspect bien particulier.

Superficies en tonos marrón y terroso caracterizan a estas cocinas, logrando así una atmósfera confortable con la misma funcionalidad. En el modelo "Pisa" (p. 68–69), las ventanas redondas características permiten una vista a los armarios y se ocupan de un aspecto inconfundible.

Le superfici, nelle tinte del marrone caldo e della terra, caratterizzano questi modelli di cucina e creano in questo modo un'atmosfera accogliente, associata ad una spiccata funzionalità. Nel modello "Pisa" (p. 68–69), i caratteristici oblò permettono di intravvedere all'interno degli armadi, donando così all'intera cucina un inconfondibile tocco di originalità.

Kornmüller

MODERN
KITCHENS

Wood in warm tones and with marked grains like beech heart wood, zebrano and teak contrast with smooth light surfaces and stainless steel or stone accents, making these kitchens truly unique. The "Ancona" model (pp. 74–75) offers something special: if required, part of the kitchen can be hidden behind an aluminum blind.

Hölzer in warmen Tönen und mit markanten Maserungen wie Kernbuche, Zebrano oder Teak kontrastieren mit glatten hellen Flächen und Akzenten aus Edelstahl oder Stein und machen die Küchen zu wahren Unikaten. Eine Besonderheit bietet das Modell „Ancona" (S. 74–75): Hinter einem Aluminiumrollo kann ein Teil der Küche bei Bedarf verborgen werden.

Des boiseries dans des tons chauds avec des veinures marquantes telles que le hêtre, le zebrano ou le teck, contrastent avec des surfaces claires et des accents d'acier inoxydable ou de la pierre pour faire de ces cuisines des pièces absolument uniques. Le modèle « Ancona » (p. 74–75) offre une particularité : une partie de la cuisine peut être cachée derrière un rideau d'aluminium si besoin est.

Las maderas en tonos cálidos y con vetas marcadas tales como haya silvestre, madera zebrano o madera de teca contrastan con superficies lisas claras y acentos de acero o piedra y convierten a las cocinas en verdaderos ejemplares únicos. El modelo "Ancona" ofrece una peculiaridad (p. 74–75): detrás de la persiana de aluminio se puede esconder una parte de la cocina si fuera necesario.

I legni, in tonalità calde e con venature marcate, quali il faggio selvatico, zebrano o teak, creano un contrasto perfetto con le superfici lisce e chiare, con note particolari in acciaio inox o pietra, rendendo così le cucine dei perfetti pezzi unici. Il modello "Ancona" (p. 74–75) propone una particolarità unica: dietro una speciale serranda in alluminio è possibile nascondere, se necessario, una parte della cucina.

Kornmüller

These kitchens lend themselves play to a modern life with increased flexibility—they offer the right setting for an opulent meal as well as for a small snack. The "Alnoart Woodglas" (pp. 76–77) range comes up with a visual novelty: the glass fronts are printed from behind with wood grain.

Einem modernen Lebensgefühl mit gesteigerter Flexibilität kommen diese Küchen entgegen – sowohl für das opulente Mahl als auch den kleinen Snack bieten sie den richtigen Rahmen. Die Serie „Alnoart Woodglas" (S. 76–77) wartet mit einer optischen Neuerung auf: Die Glasfronten sind von hinten mit Holzmaserung bedruckt.

Ces cuisines offrent un mode de vie moderne, ainsi qu'une flexibilité maximale, et offrent le cadre adapté tant pour le grand repas que pour le petit snack. La série « Alnoart Woodglas » (p. 76–77) propose une innovation optique : les vitres frontales sont imprimées de madrure à l'arrière.

A estas cocinas les conviene un estado de ánimo moderno con más flexibilidad –ofrecen el marco perfecto, tanto para la opulenta comida, como también para el pequeño refrigerio. La serie "Alnoart Woodglas" (p. 76–77) se presenta con una novedad en el aspecto: los frentes de vidrio están estampados con veteado de madera.

Queste cucine sono in grado di soddisfare la sensazione di spazio vitale moderno ad una spiccata flessibilità – per un pasto succulento, come pure per un piccolo spuntino, è dato sempre l'ambiente perfetto. La serie "Alnoart Woodglas" (p. 76–77) è realizzata con una novità estetica assoluta nel suo genere: le ante di vetro sono decorate dall'interno con le stesse venature del legno.

Alno

Anyone searching for color and variety will find it with the following kitchens. The products stand out due to a large range of colors, surfaces and materials. Open and closed storage spaces are coherently coordinated with each other and applications break things up. The "XL" model can even be individually adapted to the customer's size.

Wer auf der Suche nach Farbe und Abwechslung ist, wird bei den folgenden Küchen fündig. Die Produkte zeichnen sich durch eine große Palette an Farben, Oberflächen und Materialien aus. Offene und geschlossene Stauräume sind schlüssig aufeinander abgestimmt und Applikationen sorgen für Auflockerung. Das „XL" Modell kann sogar individuell an die Körpergröße des Kunden angepasst werden.

Celui qui recherche de la couleur et du changement, trouvera son bonheur avec ces cuisines. Les produits offrent une remarquable palette de couleurs, de surfaces et de matériaux. Des espaces de rangement ouverts et fermés sont adaptés entre eux et des applications détendent l'atmosphère. Le « XL » modèle peut même être adaptée à la taille du client.

Quien busca color y variedad, descubrirá las cocinas a continuación. Los productos destacan por la amplia paleta de colores, superficies y materiales. Los lugares abiertos y cerrados para guardar cosas coordinan de manera contundente y las aplicaciones se ocupan del aligeramiento. El "XL" modelo se puede adaptar aun individualmente a la estatura del cliente.

Chiunque cerchi il colore ed il cambiamento troverà in queste cucine ciò che fa per lui. I modelli si caratterizzano, infatti, per una vasta gamma di colori, superfici e materiali diversi. Gli spazi per riporre gli oggetti, aperti e chiusi, sono realizzati in modo convincente per la loro funzionalità e le applicazioni sono estremamente semplificate. La versione Il "XL" modello può essere addirittura adeguata alla statura corporea del Cliente.

Ballerina-Küchen

With these extremely high-quality kitchens, the innovative model B2 (pp. 96–101), alongside the classic stainless steel range B3 (pp. 102–107) and the younger range B1 (pp. 93–95), was designed by the designer company EOOS as a particularly impressive workshop for cooking: a work bench connects all preparation areas whilst separate cupboards serve as storage.

Bei diesen sehr hochwertigen Küchen überzeugt neben der klassischen Edelstahllinie B3 (S. 102–107) und der jüngeren Linie B1 (S. 93–95) besonders das innovative Modell B2 (S. 96–101), das von dem Designbüro EOOS als Werkstatt zum Kochen konzipiert wurde: eine Werkbank kombiniert alle Bereiche für die Zubereitung, während separate Schränke der Aufbewahrung dienen.

Parmi ces cuisines de qualité et à côté de la ligne B3 (p. 102–107) classique en acier inoxydable et de la ligne B1 (p. 93–95) plus jeune, le modèle innovant B2 (p. 96–101) est particulièrement convaincant. Il a été créé par le bureau de design EOOS et conçu comme un atelier pour cuisiner : un banc d'outils combine tous les domaines de la préparation, tandis que des placards séparés servent au rangement.

En estas cocinas de muy alta calidad convence, además de la línea clásica B3 (p. 102–107) de acero inoxidable y de la línea más joven B1 (p. 93–95), el modelo innovador B2 (p. 96–101), concebido por el estudio de diseño EOOS como taller para cocinar: un banco de trabajo combina todas las áreas para la preparación, mientras que los armarios sirven para guardar cosas.

In queste cucine preziose convince, oltre alla linea classica in acciaio inox B3 (p. 102–107) e alla linea più giovane B1 (p. 93–95), soprattutto l'innovativo modello B2 (p. 96–101), concepito dall'agenzia di design EOOS, nella forma di un'officina per la preparazione di pietanze: un vero e proprio banco da lavoro unisce tutte le aree per la preparazione degli alimenti, mentre la loro conservazione è permessa grazie agli armadi separati.

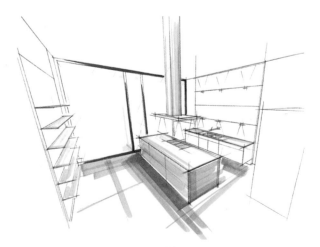

Bulthaup

The colors black, white and grey as well as brushed stainless steel define the professional, minimalist look and feel of the kitchens shown here. Their look and fittings are aimed at the ambitious amateur chef who has superior demands on functionality and robustness.

Die Farben Schwarz, Weiß und Grau sowie gebürsteter Edelstahl definieren die professionelle, puristische Anmutung der hier abgebildeten Küchen. Diese richten sich in Optik und Ausstattung an den ambitionierten Hobbykoch, der gehobene Ansprüche an die Funktionalität und Robustheit stellt.

Les couleurs noir, blanc et gris, ainsi que de l'acier inoxydable brossé définissent l'aspect professionnel et puriste de ces cuisines. Celles-ci, de par leur optique et leur équipement, s'adaptent aux cuisiniers amateurs ambitieux et à leurs exigences de fonctionnalité et de robustesse.

Los colores negro, blanco y gris, así como el acero inoxidable cepillado, definen el aspecto purista y profesional de las cocinas mostradas aquí. El aspecto y el equipamiento de las mismas están dirigidos al cocinero aficionado ambicioso, quien tiene altas exigencias para la funcionalidad y robustez.

Le superfici nei colori nero, bianco e grigio, insieme all'acciaio inox in versione spazzolata, accentuano la particolarità puristica delle cucine qui raffigurate. Nell'aspetto e nella dotazione, queste cucine si orientano particolarmente ad un ambizioso cuoco per passione, il quale abbia notevoli esigenze di funzionalità e robustezza per la sua cucina.

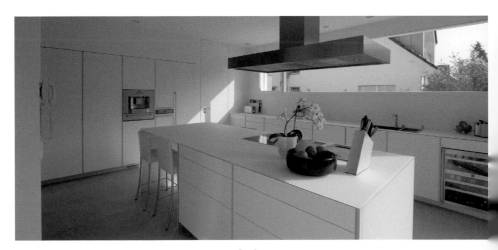

Cucina

These models are modern, functional and affordable, and can be put together by the customer according to their personal needs. Tables can be used for eating, storage and preparation, open and closed systems serve as storage space and modules can be combined in various different ways. Flexibility is the key.

Modern, funktional und erschwinglich sind diese Modelle, die sich der Kunde nach seinen persön-lichen Bedürfnissen zusammenstellen kann. Tische können zum Essen, Aufbewahren und Zubereiten verwendet werden, offene und geschlossene Systeme dienen als Stauräume, Module können vielfältig kombiniert werden. Flexibilität wird groß geschrieben.

Ces modèles sont modernes, fonctionnels et abordables, et peuvent être assemblés par le client selon ses propres besoins. Les tables peuvent être utilisées pour manger, conserver et préparer, des systèmes ouverts et fermés servent d'espaces de rangement, des modules peuvent être combinés de diverses façons. Flexibilité prend une majuscule avec ces cuisines.

Estos modelos son modernos, funcionales y asequibles, los cuales el cliente puede componer según sus necesidades personales. Las mesas se pueden utilizar para comer, almacenar y preparar, los sistemas abiertos y cerrados sirven para guardar cosas, los módulos se pueden combinar de manera múltiple. La flexibilidad es muy importante.

Questi modelli, moderni, funzionali e convenienti, possono essere composti insieme dal Cliente, secondo le sue esigenze personali. I tavoli possono essere impiegati per mangiare, conservare e preparare le pietanze, i sistemi aperti e chiusi sono perfetti per riporre gli oggetti; infine, i moduli possono essere combinati insieme con la massima versatilità. La flessibilità strutturale raggiunge così il suo apice.

IKEA

In the "Modern Purism" product range the manufacturer places great importance on clean lines, geometrical surfaces and the subtle use of materials, inspired by functional Bauhaus design. The "P'7340" (pp. 127–129) model, which was developed together with Porsche Design and stands out due to its technical look and feel is particularly exclusive.

In der Produktlinie „Moderner Purismus" legt der Hersteller Wert auf klare Linien, geometrische Flächen und dezenten Materialeinsatz, inspiriert durch das funktionale Design des Bauhauses. Besonders exklusiv ist das Modell „P'7340" (S. 127–129), das zusammen mit Porsche Design entwickelt wurde und durch seine technoide Anmutung besticht.

Dans la ligne de produits « Moderner Purismus », le fabricant mise sur des lignes claires, des surfaces géométriques et une utilisation décente des matériaux, inspiré par le design fonctionnel du Bauhaus. Le modèle « P'7340 » (p. 127–129) élaboré en collaboration avec Porche Design est particulièrement raffiné et imprégné d'un aspect technoïde.

En la línea de productos „purismo moderno", el fabricante les da importancia a las líneas claras, a superficies geométricas y al uso decente del material, inspirado en el diseño funcional del estilo Bauhaus. El modelo "P'7340" (p. 127–129) es especialmente exclusivo, y fue desarrollado junto con la empresa Porsche Design y fascina gracias a su aspecto tecnoide.

Nella linea di prodotti "Purismo moderno", è evidente che questo costruttore di cucine tiene particolarmente alle linee chiare, alle superfici geometriche e all'impiego di materiali definiti, ispirato dal design funzionale della scuola di Bauhaus. Particolarmente esclusivo è il modello "P'7340" (p. 127–129), realizzato insieme al Porsche Design e con un caratteristico accento tecnologico.

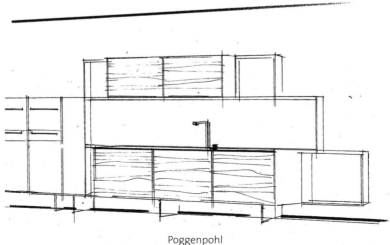

Poggenpohl

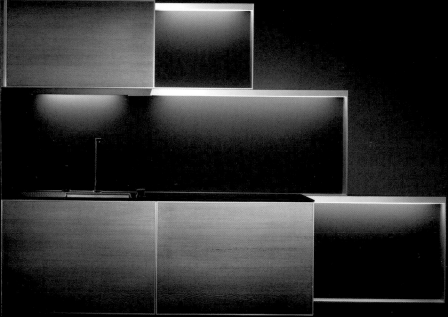

Modern Kitchens

With a warm, soft look and feel and many features from the furniture industry, these products merge directly into the living space. The "Emotion" (pp. 140–143) model with its stainless steel runners and different height levels translates this concept particularly consistently.

Mit einer warmen, weichen Anmutung und vielen Merkmalen aus dem Möbelbereich verschmelzen diese Produkte direkt mit dem Wohnraum. Besonders das Modell „Emotion" (S. 140–143) mit seinen Edelstahlkufen und unterschiedlichen Höhenabstufungen setzt dieses Konzept konsequent um.

Avec un aspect chaleureux et doux et de nombreuses caractéristiques tirées du mobilier, ces produits se fondent directement dans le salon. Le modèle « Emotion » (p. 140–143) avec ses patins en acier inoxydable et ses niveaux de hauteurs variés présente particulièrement bien le concept.

Con un aspecto cálido suave y varias características del sector de los muebles, estos productos se fusionan directamente con la sala de estar. Este modelo hace realidad este concepto consecuentemente, especialmente el modelo "Emotion" (p. 140–143) con sus patas tipo patín y las más diversas graduaciones de altura.

Grazie ad una nota calda e morbida e alle numerose caratteristiche dal mondo dell'arredamento, questi modelli si fondono perfettamente alla zona giorno. In particolare, il modello "Emotion", (p. 140–143) con le sue superfici in acciaio inox ed i suoi diversi livelli di altezza, concretizza con coerenza tale concetto.

rational

The following kitchens stand out due to good organization and well-thought through details. The "S1" (pp. 150–151) model features a special highlight: various modern media can be integrated from TV to Internet and sophisticated light controls provide the right mood—everything controlled by one interactive user interface.

Gute Organisation und durchdachte Details zeichnen die folgenden Küchen aus. Ein besonderes Highlight stellt das Modell „S1" (S. 150–151) dar: von TV bis Internet lassen sich vielfältige moderne Medien integrieren und eine ausgefeilte Lichtsteuerung sorgt für die richtige Stimmung – alles reguliert über eine interaktive Bedienoberfläche.

Une bonne organisation et des détails bien pensés caractérisent ces cuisines. Le modèle « S1 » (p. 150–151) est le summum : de la télévision à internet, de nombreux médias modernes y sont intégrés, et un système de commande lumineux soigné produit l'atmosphère adéquate. Et le tout est commandé à partir d'un écran interactif.

La buena organización y los detalles bien meditados distinguen a las cocinas a continuación. El modelo "S1" (p. 150–151) presenta un especto especial interesante: desde televisión hasta internet se pueden integrar múltiples medios de comunicación modernos y un control de la iluminación se ocupa del ambiente correcto –todo está regulado mediante una superficie de operación interactiva.

La perfetta organizzazione ed i dettagli elaborati delineano i seguenti modelli di cucina. Una versione speciale è sicuramente il modello "S1" (p. 150–151): dal televisore al collegamento a internet, queste cucine possono essere integrate con tutti i comfort mediatici moderni; inoltre, la raffinata regolazione delle luci permette di ottenere sempre l'atmosfera perfetta – il tutto regolato attraverso un telecomando interattivo.

SieMatic

152   Modern Kitchens

Timeless kitchens of high craftsmanship, which fulfill individual customer requirements, are manufactured from precious solid woods from sustainable forestry. Special details, for example an electrical fully height adjustable worktop, take this concept into account.

Mit edlen Massivhölzern aus nachhaltiger Forstwirtschaft werden zeitlose Küchen von hoher handwerklicher Qualität gefertigt, die den individuellen Ansprüchen des Kunden gerecht werden. Besondere Details, wie zum Beispiel eine elektrisch- stufenlos höhenverstellbare Arbeitsplatte tragen diesem Konzept Rechnung.

Des cuisines intemporelles de grande qualité artisanale, qui remplissent les attentes des clients, peuvent être réalisées à partir de bois massif de foresteries durables. Des détails particuliers, tels que le réglage électrique sans cran de la hauteur constituent les avantages de ce concept.

Con maderas macizas finas de explotación forestal duradera se fabrican cocinas independientemente de la moda de alta calidad artesanal, las cuales cumplen con las exigencias individuales del cliente. Los detalles especiales, como por ejemplo, una mesa de trabajo regulable eléctricamente a cualquier altura, consideran este concepto.

Dai preziosi legni massicci derivati da una concezione boschiva sostenibile vengono realizzate delle cucine senza tempo, caratterizzate da una qualità artigianale eccezionale, in grado di soddisfare anche le massime esigenze. I dettagli particolari, quali il piano di lavoro a regolazione continua elettrica per l'altezza, testimoniano questa filosofia strutturale.

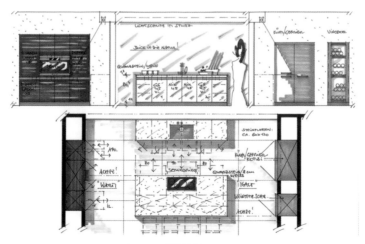

TEAM 7

Simply cooking was yesterday—today a variety of preparation is used. Alongside cooking and baking these include steaming, grilling or frying. Programmable ovens support preparation and combination equipment can bake and cook "au gratin" at the same time.

Einfach nur kochen war gestern – heutzutage kommt eine Vielzahl von Zubereitungsarten zum Einsatz. Neben Kochen und Backen sind dies etwa Dampfgaren, Grillen oder Frittieren. Programmierbare Backöfen unterstützen bei der Zubereitung und Kombigeräte können zeitgleich kochen und gratinieren.

Simplement cuisiner, c'est du passer. Aujourd'hui, de nombreuses sortes de préparation entrent en jeu. Parallèlement à cuisiner et mijoter, il faut également cuire à la vapeur, griller ou faire frire. Des fours programmables aident à la préparation et des appareils combinés sont capables de faire cuire et de gratiner en même temps.

Cocinar solamente, fue ayer –hoy en día se realizan varios tipos de preparaciones. Además de cocinar y hornear, son a saber cocinar a vapor, a la parrilla o freir. Los hornos programables ayudan en la preparación y los aparatos combinados pueden cocinar y gratinar a la vez.

Semplicemente cucinare è una concezione che appartiene ormai al passato – oggi devono essere invece possibili moltissimi tipi di preparazioni diverse. Oltre a cucinare ed infornare, la cucina moderna esige anche la cottura a vapore, la griglia e la frittura. I forni programmabili sono degli ausili efficienti per la preparazione e gli elettrodomestici combinati sono in grado di cucinare e gratinare allo stesso tempo.

Cooking

As wonderful as the food might smell—the smell should not spread throughout the whole house. Modern extractor hoods efficiently direct steam and smells outside. Placed free-standing in the room they remind you of a traditional chimney flue. Stainless steel models are easy to clean and professional looking.

So gut das Essen auch duften mag – der Geruch soll sich nicht allzu sehr im Haus verbreiten. Moderne Dunstabzugshauben leiten Dampf und Gerüche effizient nach außen. Frei im Raum platziert erinnern sie an einen traditionellen Kaminabzug. Edelstahlmodelle sind pflegeleicht und verleihen ein professionelles Aussehen.

Certes, la nourriture sent très bon, mais cette odeur ne doit pas se répandre dans toute la maison. Les hottes d'aération modernes évacuent efficacement les vapeurs et les odeurs vers l'extérieur. Placées librement dans la pièce, elles évoquent une hotte de cheminée traditionnelle. Les modèles en acier inoxydable sont faciles d'entretien et offrent un aspect professionnel.

Como quiera que huela bien la comida —el olor no se debe propagar tanto en toda la casa. Las campanas extractoras de cocina modernas conducen el vapor y los olores de manera eficiente hacia afuera. Colocadas libremente en el ambiente, hacen recordar a una campana de chimenea. Los modelos de acero inoxidable son fáciles de cuidar y dan un aspecto profesional.

La buona cucina può profumare quanto vuole – l'odore non deve però espandersi in tutta la casa. Le cappe aspiranti moderne deviano all'esterno il vapore di cottura e gli odori da essa derivati. Sistemate libere nell'ambiente, ricordano la tradizionale cappa fumaria di un camino. I modelli in acciaio inox sono di facile cura e donano un aspetto professionale all'intero complesso.

Exhaust Hoods

The latest fridges and freezers do their jobs while remaining extremely sophisticated: they have intelligent electronic controls, water and ice dispensers as well as different temperature zones for different foods—even your wine has its own section at a suitable temperature.

Aktuelle Kühl- und Gefrierschränke verrichten ihren Dienst äußerst raffiniert: Sie verfügen über eine ausgeklügelte elektronische Steuerung, Wasser- und Eisspender sowie verschiedene Temperaturzonen für unterschiedliche Lebensmittel – so findet auch ein edler Tropfen sein eigens temperiertes Fach.

Les réfrigérateurs actuels effectuent leur tâche de façon particulièrement raffinée : ils disposent d'une commande électronique sophistiquée, de robinets d'eau et de distributeurs de glace, ainsi que de diverses zones de température pour les différents types de nourriture. Ainsi, chaque précieux vin trouve son emplacement tempéré.

Todos los frigoríficos y congeladores cumplen con su trabajo de manera extraordinariamente refinada: tienen un control electrónico sofisticado, distribuidor de agua y de hielo, así como diferentes zonas de temperatura para diferentes alimentos —así un vino fino también tiene su propio compartimiento temperado.

Gli apparecchi frigorifero-congelatore svolgono la loro funzione con la massima raffinatezza: sono dotati di un elaborato sistema di comando elettronico; dosatore per l'acqua e per il ghiaccio, insieme a diverse zone di temperatura per alimenti differenti – così, anche un vino pregiato può trovare il suo vano di temperatura perfetta.

Fridges

Whether it's a chopping board, bread bin, spice rack, or herb pot—the right accessories finish off the kitchen and make work a piece of cake. The functional and beautiful aids are indispensable for the room's harmonious overall image and the professional preparation of meals.

Ob Schneidebrett, Brotbox, Gewürzdose oder Kräutertopf – die richtigen Accessoires machen die Küche erst komplett und lassen die Arbeit leicht von der Hand gehen. Für ein stimmiges Gesamtbild des Raumes und eine professionelle Zubereitung der Speisen sind die funktionalen und schönen Helfer unverzichtbar.

Qu'il s'agisse d'une planche à découper, d'une corbeille à pain, de boîtes à épices ou de pots à herbes, ce sont les accessoires adéquats qui parachèvent la cuisine et rendent le travail facile à effectuer. Pour une image convenable de la pièce et une préparation professionnelle des plats, il est impossible de se priver de ces aides fonctionnelles et esthétiques.

Ya sea la tabla de cortar, la caja para el pan, la lata de especias o la maceta de hierbas –los accesorios correctos completan recién la cocina y facilitan el trabajo. Los ayudantes funcionales y bellos son indispensables para una visión de conjunto armónica del ambiente y una preparación profesional de las comidas.

Il tagliere, la scatola dello spuntino, il contenitore delle spezie o il vaso delle erbe fresche – solo gli accessori giusti rendono la cucina completa e possono facilitare notevolmente il lavoro. Per un'immagine armoniosa dell'ambiente e una preparazione professionale delle pietanze, gli ausili in cucina funzionali e pregevoli nell'aspetto sono veramente indispensabili.

Accessories

Kitchen manufacturers know: only clearly laid out kitchens can be well managed. Therefore, they offer large and small solutions for storage which create order. Alternating between open and closed areas makes planning easier and brings visuals to life.

Die Küchenhersteller wissen: Nur in einer übersichtlichen Küche lässt es sich gut wirtschaften. Daher bieten sie große und kleine Lösungen zur Aufbewahrung, die für Ordnung sorgen. Eine Abwechslung von offenen und geschlossenen Bereichen erleichtert die Planung und belebt die Optik.

Les fabricants de cuisine le savent : seule une cuisine bien organisée est facile à gérer. C'est pourquoi ils proposent de grandes et petites solutions de rangement assurant un bon ordre. Une variation d'espaces ouverts et fermés facilite la planification et rend l'aspect plus vivant.

Los fabricantes de cocinas saben: solamente en una cocina con buena disposición se puede llevar la casa. Por eso ofrecen soluciones grandes y pequeñas para el almacenamiento, las cuales se ocupan del orden. Una variedad de áreas cerradas y abiertas facilita la planificación y estimula el aspecto.

I costruttori di cucine lo sanno bene: solo una cucina facile da gestire può essere utile. Per questo, vi sono qui soluzioni piccole e grandi per spazi porta-oggetti, in grado di creare l'ordine perfetto. L'alternanza di settori aperti e chiusi facilita la pianificazione e ravviva l'aspetto dell'intero complesso.

Storage

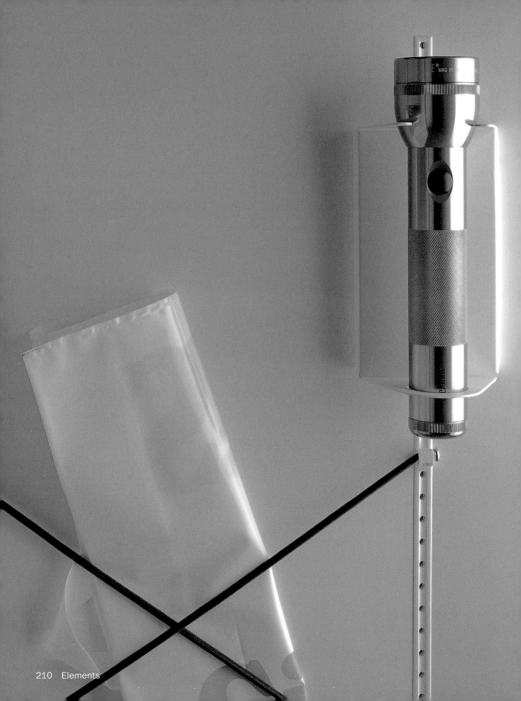

This modern dining desk serves as a dining table and a worktable at the same time and allows a smooth fusion of preparing, serving and eating. The cutlery can be found in the cutlery drawer integrated into the table, stainless steel trolleys for meals and drinks can be integrated directly into the table.

Dieser moderne Esstisch dient gleichzeitig als Ess- und Arbeitstisch und erlaubt eine fließende Verbindung von Zubereitung, Servieren und Essen. Das Besteck findet sich in einem in den Tisch installierten Besteckkasten, Edelstahl-Trolleys für Speisen und Getränke können direkt in die Tafel integriert werden.

Cette desserte moderne sert tant de table à manger que de plan de travail et permet un enchaîne-ment rapide entre la préparation, le service et le repas. Les couverts trouveront leur place dans un bac à couverts incorporé dans la table et des charriots en acier inoxydable pour les repas et les boissons peuvent y être directement intégrés.

Esta mesa de comer moderna sirve como mesa de comer y de trabajo a la vez y permite un enlace fluido de preparación, servir y comer. Los cubiertos se encuentran en una caja de cubiertos empotrado en la mesa, los carritos de acero inoxidable para comidas y bebidas se pueden integrar directamente en la mesa.

Questo moderno Dining Desk funge contemporaneamente da tavola da pranzo e piano di lavoro, permettendo così l'unione perfetta tra la preparazione, il servizio e la consumazione dei pasti. Le posate sono riposte in un cassetto apposito instalaro al tavolo, i carrelli in acciaio inox per le pietanze e le bevande possono essere integrati direttamente al tavolo.

Dining Desk

Miele & Cie. KG
Carl-Miele-Straße 29
33332 Gütersloh
Germany
Phone: +49 / 5241 / 890
Fax: +49 / 5241 / 89 20 90
info@miele.de
www.miele.de

Poggenpohl Möbelwerke GmbH
Poggenpohlstraße 1
32051 Herford
Germany
Phone: +49 / 5221 / 38 10
Fax: +49 / 5221 / 38 13 21
info@poggenpohl.com
www.poggenpohl.com

rational einbauküchen GmbH
Rationalstraße 4
49328 Melle
Germany
Phone: +49 / 5226 / 580
Fax: +49 / 5226 / 582 12
info@rational.de
www.rational.de

SieMatic Deutschland
SieMatic Möbelwerke
GmbH & Co. KG
August-Siekmann-Straße 1–5
32584 Löhne
Germany
Phone: +49 / 5732 / 670
Fax: +49 / 5732 / 672 97
info@siematic.de
www.siematic.com

TEAM 7 Natürlich Wohnen GmbH
Braunauer Straße 26
4910 Ried i.I.
Austria
Phone: +43 / 7752 / 97 70
Fax: +43 / 7752 / 97 77 77
info@team7.at
www.team7.at

Other titles by teNeues

ISBN 978-3-8327-9343-2

ISBN 978-3-8327-9342-5

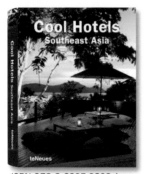

ISBN 978-3-8327-9308-1

ISBN 978-3-8327-9309-8

ISBN 978-3-8327-9307-4

ISBN 978-3-8327-9323-4

Size: **15 x 19 cm**, 6 x 7½ in., 224 pp., **Flexicover**, c. 200 color photographs,
Text: English / German / French / Spanish / Italian

www.teneues.com